Analogue Guide

Paris

Contents

Paris

—Welcome to Analogue Paris

Clouded in perfume and with a penchant for champagne and the good things in life, Paris is the *grande dame* of world cities. As the sophisticated, Continental counterpart to dynamic New York and quirky London, the city has been a fixture on the high calibre circuit in all disciplines for generations.

Paris dates back to 250 BC when the Parisii, a Celtic tribe, established a fishing village on the river Seine. The Romans subsequently founded the settlement of Lutetia on the site, which was later renamed Paris. The city consolidated its role as the capital of the powerful Frankish empire that reigned over much of Western Europe under Charlemagne. During the Age of Enlightenment, Paris became the centre of the intellectual world for more than two centuries: the home of new literary and artistic movements and the cradle of the language of diplomacy—all set within the scintillating splendour of gilded domes, fussily manicured gardens and a deep-rooted *joie de vivre*. In the minds of many Parisians this period still continues, even though the avant-garde has moved on to New York, London and Berlin, threatening to leave Paris on the sidelines of history.

More recently, Paris has embraced the challenge of transposing its glittering past into the future, diversifying away from the spending of Asian tourists and American expats. Holding on to its prized credentials of luxury and romance, the city has opened itself to the world and even to its peripheral suburbs. We have ventured to uncover what 21st century Paris has to offer—from ebullient *bars à vins* and glam boutiques in the first arrondissement to rustic home cooking in the twentieth. Enjoy!

Neighbourhoods

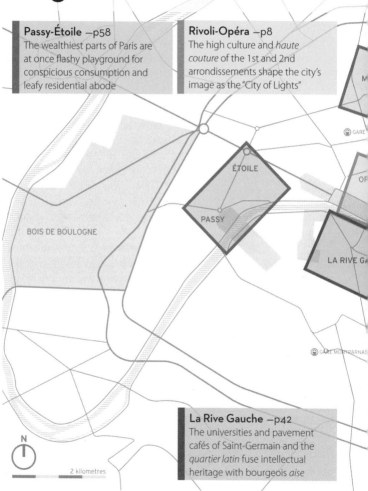

Passy-Étoile —p58
The wealthiest parts of Paris are at once flashy playground for conspicuous consumption and leafy residential abode

Rivoli-Opéra —p8
The high culture and *haute couture* of the 1st and 2nd arrondissements shape the city's image as the "City of Lights"

BOIS DE BOULOGNE

ÉTOILE

PASSY

LA RIVE GA

GARE

OP

GARE MONTPARNAS

La Rive Gauche —p42
The universities and pavement cafés of Saint-Germain and the *quartier latin* fuse intellectual heritage with bourgeois *aise*

N

2 kilometres

Montmartre & Pigalle —p88
Despite its popular appeal, Montmartre has retained much of its charm and is still home to a vibrant creative community

St-Denis-République —p64
Historically home to the working class, today the area is a melting pot of recent immigrants and young professionals

Le Marais —p24
The "swamp" has played host to clergy and nobility, Jewish traders, gay nightlife and more recently, galleries and boutiques

La Bastille —p78
Beyond the hubbub of the Place de la Bastille, this mostly residential area is interspersed with beautiful squares and culinary highlights

GARE DU NORD

GARE DE L'EST

FAUBOURG ST-DENIS

RÉPUBLIQUE

OBERKAMPF

LE MARAIS

LA BASTILLE

GARE DE LYON

GARE AUSTERLITZ

BOIS DE VINCENNES

ORLY (10KM)

Rivoli-Opéra

—Royal Glamour and Republican Reality Side by Side

Paris' first and second arrondissements play an important part in shaping the city's image as the "City of Lights". The area is dotted with elegant architecture, most famously the Louvre and Notre-Dame cathedral. The rue Saint-Honoré and nearby Place Vendôme brim with high culture and *haute couture*. The bustle fades away beyond the Palais Royal, where, as if by magic, lies a tranquil oasis complete with small ateliers and informal brasseries.

At the same time, Paris' historical centre is one of the most diverse parts of this world city. Across the rue du Louvre, just steps away from the high-end boutiques, lies the city's beating heart: Châtelet. For eight centuries, the area was dominated by the *Les Halles* wholesale food market, which Emile Zola famously called "the belly of Paris". In the 1970s, the market was replaced with a gigantic transport interchange and underground shopping mall . Though widely loathed and now finally being remodelled, *Les Halles'* easy accessibility from the city's periphery injects a dose of diversity into this otherwise decidedly upmarket part of Paris. Just adjacent to the former market, the small pedestrianised streets of the *quartier de l'horloge* around rue de Montorgueil reflect the democratic character of the area.

At the northern edge of the second arrondissement, the city centre's charms give way to the *grands boulevards* laid out by Baron Haussmann in the late 19th century. In the west, near the lavish Opéra Garnier and the Saint-Lazare station, lies Paris' upmarket commercial district, boasting private banks, fashion boutiques and department stores. In the east, towards République (p64), the boulevards acquire a grittier and more diverse feel; this is where one finds most of the city's surviving 19th century glazed commercial arcades, now dominated by coin collectors and antique shops.

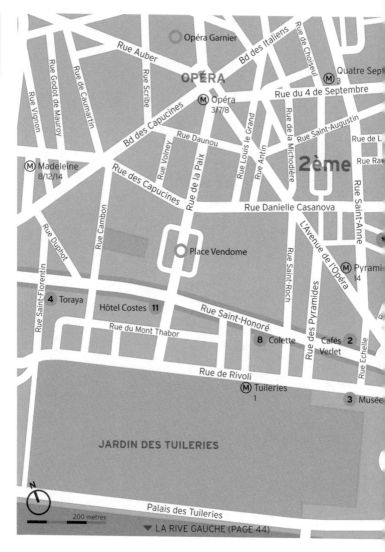

Opéra Garnier

Rue Auber

Bd des Italiens

Rue de Choiseul

OPÉRA

Quatre Sept
3

M Opéra
3/7/8

Rue du 4 de Septembre

Rue Godot de Mauroy

Rue de Caumartin

Rue Scribe

Rue Vignon

Bd des Capucines

Rue Daunou

Rue Louis le Grand

Rue de la Michodière

Rue Saint-Augustin

Rue de L

M Madeleine
8/12/14

Rue des Capucines

Rue Volney

Rue de la Paix

Rue Antin

2ème

Rue Ra

Rue Cambon

Rue des Capucines

Rue Danielle Casanova

Rue Saint-Anne

Rue Duphot

Rue Saint-Florentin

Place Vendome

Rue Saint-Roch

L'Avenue de l'Opéra

M Pyrami
14

4 Toraya

Hôtel Costes 11

Rue Saint-Honoré

Rue de Pyramides

8 Colette

Cafés 2
Verlet

Rue Échelle

Rue du Mont Thabor

Rue de Rivoli

M Tuileries
1

3 Musée

JARDIN DES TUILERIES

N

200 metres

Palais des Tuileries

▼ LA RIVE GAUCHE (PAGE 44)

▲ ST-DENIS-RÉPUBLIQUE (PAGE 66)

Rue du Caire

Rue Feydeau

Bourse
3
Ⓜ

Rue du Croissant

Rue Saint-Joseph

10 Le Frenchie

Rue Notre-Dame-des-Victoires

Rue Montmartre

Rue de Cléry

Ⓜ Sentier
3

Rue Reaumur

Pl de la Bourse

Rue P. Lelong

Rue du Mail

Rue d'Aboukir

Colbert

Rue de la Banque

QUARTIER DE L'HORLOGE

Rue Vivienne

Passage du Grand-Cerf **7**

Rue Montmartre

Rue Tiquetonne

PALAIS ROYAL

ue des Petits Champs

Rue Hérold

Rue Étienne Marcel

Étienne Marcel Ⓜ
4

Rue Jean-Jacques Rousseau

Rue de Turbigo

▶ LE MARAIS (PAGE 26)

pe

JARDIN DU
PALAIS ROYAL

Rue de Valois

Rue Croix des Petits Champs

Rue du Bouloi

Rue du Louvre

Ⓜ Les Halles
4

Les Halles Ⓞ

Rue du Colonel Driant

Le Palais Royal Ⓞ

6 L'Atelier du Pélican

Rue Berger

Rue Saint-Honoré

Rue Saint-Honoré

Rue du Roule

Rue des Halles

RIVOLI

1er

Décoratifs

Ⓜ

Palais Royal-Musée du Louvre
1/7

Rue de Rivoli

Ⓜ Louvre-Rivoli
1

9 Le Fumoir

Rue du Pont Neuf

Rue des Bourdonnais

Musée du Louvre Ⓞ

Kong **5**

Pont Neuf Ⓜ
7

Rue Bertin Poirée

Quai François Mitterrand

▼ LA RIVE GAUCHE (PAGE 45)

LA SEINE

Caffeinated Excellence

Télescope

1 5 Rue Villedo
+33 1 42 61 33 14
telescopecafe.com
Ⓜ Pyramides **7** **14**, Palais Royal-
Musée du Louvre **1** **7**, Quatre-
Septembre **3**
Closed Sun. Open Mon-Fri 8.30am-
5pm; Sat 9.30am-6.30pm

In a city crammed full of cafés, the relative scarcity of espresso-based excellence can be somewhat surprising. Télescope bucks the trend, achieving the pinnacle of artisanal caffeination at its bijou sized café and roastery. A gleaming La Marzocco machine, topped with pristine blue and white cups, sits handsomely atop a solid wood bar, where patrons placidly leaf through the pages of Le Parisien. After indulging in the café's refined simplicity, head out for a refreshing stroll around the nearby *jardins du Palais Royal* or pop into one of the largely Japanese area's delectable ramen, udon or sushi shops.

A Cup with a Past

Cafés et Thés Verlet

2 256 Rue Saint-Honoré
+33 1 42 60 67 39
cafesverlet.com
Ⓜ Palais Royal-Musée du
Louvre **1** **7**, Pyramides **7** **14**
Closed Sun. Open Mon-Sat 9.30am-
6.30pm (shop until 7pm)

Founded in 1880 by seafarer Auguste Whoehré, Verlet soon became a prime location for sourcing exquisite and exotic rice, spices, tea and a spattering of coffee. Whoehré's grandson Pierre Verlet took over in 1965, gradually building a coffee repertoire worthy of the serious connoisseur. Now owned by coffee expert Eric Duchossoy, who bought the business from Verlet, the café and roaster is a destination for those seeking the perfectly curated cup or the aromatic delights of over fifty loose-leaf teas.

Fashion and Design Temple

Musée des Arts Décoratifs

3 107 Rue de Rivoli
+33 1 44 55 57 50
lesartsdecoratifs.fr

Ⓜ Palais Royal-Musée du Louvre ①
⑦, Pyramides ⑦ ⑭, Tuileries ①
Closed Mon. Open Tue-Sun 11am-6pm; Thu temporary exhibitions until 9pm

The "Arts Décoratifs" is a bastion of decorative arts, design, textiles, fashion and graphism. Recent highlights include an exploration of the "underworld" of male and female undergarments used to stylise the body into the ideal beauty of different epochs, and an in-depth exploration of French graphic designer Philippe Apeloig's creative process across the typographic spectrum. The museum's shop offers a vast range of fascinating design related books and objects. And for a succulent taste of French decorative art history, visit the museum's sister site, le musée Nissim de Camondo.

Wagashi sur Seine

Toraya

(4) 10 Rue Saint-Florentin
+33 1 42 60 13 00
toraya-group.co.jp
Ⓜ Concorde ① ⑧ ⑫,
Pyramides ⑧ ⑫ ⑭
Closed Sun. Open Mon-Sat 10.30am-7pm

Japanese confectioner Toraya's intricate and visually exquisite *wagashi*, or Japanese confections, first hit the *hexagone* in 1980 with the opening of its Paris shop and tearoom. The shop's warm wood panelling, coral and cream armchairs and black lacquered accoutrements plunge the guest into a tantalising mix of Japanese bubble economy era bling and Gallic *je ne sais quoi*. Settle in for a perfectly frothed bowl of *matcha* accompanied by a delicately moist *dora yaki* cake or opt for an impeccably served light lunch before hitting the shops.

A Bar with a View

Kong

5 1 Rue du Pont Neuf
+33 1 40 39 09 00
kong.fr
Ⓜ Pont Neuf ⑦, Châtelet ① ④ ⑦ ⑪ ⑭
Open daily 12.15pm-midnight; Fri/Sat
bar 10pm-3am

A Philippe Starck designed adventure in the sky with Japanese accents, restaurant/bar Kong offers spectacular city views from its glass domed rooftop perch atop Kenzo's Paris offices. Pop by for a *coupe de champagne* or settle in for an evening of fusion cuisine beneath the stars. Afterwards, hit the neighbourhood's *boîtes branchées* or popping into Hôtel Costes (p22) for a late night cocktail.

Cardboard Creations
L'Atelier du Pélican

6 10 Rue du Pélican
+33 1 42 86 01 36
atelierdupelican.com

Ⓜ Louvre-Rivoli ❶ ❼, Palais Royal-
Musée du Louvre ❶ ❼

Closed Sun. Open Mon 2pm-7pm;
Tue-Fri 11am-7pm; Sat 2pm-8pm

An architect with a passion for
recovered materials, cardboard
in particular, Claude Jeantet first
opened her atelier-boutique in
1998. Today her whimsical and
ludic inventions take on the form
of animals, frames, boxes and
box-animals, all to be beheld
and purchased at L'Atelier du
Pélican. Courses in cardboard
creation, architectural drawing and
watercolour painting are offered
throughout the year.

© Jacky Corbel

Elegant Passage

Passage du Grand-Cerf

7 between Rue Dussoubs and Rue Saint-Denis

Ⓜ Étienne Marcel ❹, Réaumur - Sébastopol ❸❹

Open daily 8.30am-8pm

Nothing could be more Parisian than the blend of elegance and shopping provided by its passages. Around 150 of these shopping arcades were created in the late 18th century, but many were destroyed by Haussmann's broad boulevards or made obsolete by the new *grands magasins*. Most of the remaining 25 passages lead a sidelined existence as home to antique merchants and philatelists' shops. The Passage du Grand-Cerf, however, with its carefully refurbished tiles, glass ceiling and ironwork, is lined with small designer and jewellery shops and is now a retail destination.

Parfum to Perrier

Colette

8 213 Rue Saint-Honoré
+33 1 55 35 33 90
colette.fr
Ⓜ Tuileries ①, Pyramides ⑦⑭
Closed Sun. Open Mon-Sat 11am-7pm

Hip, sophisticated, and minimalist, lifestyle concept store Colette is contemporary Paris' answer to the traditional *grand magasin* department store. This bijou emporium boasts a curated selection of the latest *tendances* in everything from fashion to books and furniture. And if all that heady *parfum* sampling has clouded your senses, proceed to the subterranean water-bar, where you can sober up with over 70 varieties of H_2O.

Grog and Intellect

Le Fumoir

9 6 Rue de l'Amiral de Coligny
+33 1 42 92 00 24
lefumoir.com
Ⓜ Louvre-Rivoli **1** **7**, Pont Neuf **7**
Open daily 11am-2am

A plush and glamorous *adresse*, Le Fumoir is a Parisian watering hole offering equal doses of intellect and elegance. Plush banquettes and a wooden bar—salvaged from a Chicago speakeasy—complement the café/bar's majestic setting in an elegant building worthy of the neighbouring Louvre. While this is certainly the perfect spot to while away a wintery evening over a *grog au rhum*, Le Fumoir doubles as a prime breakfast café where you can enjoy your croissant with a good selection of international press and books on offer to patrons.

Affable Frenchie

Le Frenchie

10 5-6 Rue du Nil
+33 1 40 39 96 19
frenchie-restaurant.com
Ⓜ Sentier ③, Bonne Nouvelle ⑧
Closed Sat/Sun
Restaurant: Mon-Fri services at 7pm
and 9.30pm (reservation only)
Bar: Open Mon-Fri 7pm-11pm (no
reservations)

Hidden down a small cobbled street amidst the textile workshops of Le Sentier, tiny gastronomic and oenological powerhouse Le Frenchie, and its wine bar cousin across the street, offer laid-back cuisine and particularly interesting small producer bottles in an affable, medieval setting. Frenchie assembles an international blend of chefs, sommeliers and whisky specialists at once supremely well versed in their respective arts and refreshingly *sympathiques*. The venue's name has its origins as Executive Chef Gregory Marchand's nickname, garnered while working under Jamie Oliver at London's *Fifteen*.

Bling and Intrigue

Hôtel Costes

11 239 Rue Saint-Honoré
+33 1 42 44 50 00
hotelcostes.com
Ⓜ Tuileries **1**, Madelaine **8 12 14**
Bar: Open daily 5pm-2am
Doubles from €600/night incl. tax

Redolent of baroque-noir and beloved by the chic nightlife set, Hôtel Costes' dimly lit and palm dotted bar sets the ultimate scene for a clandestine encounter over a *kir royal*. Resident DJ Stéphane Pampougnac's loungy soundtrack wafts in the background, setting the tone for an evening of mystery and intrigue on upscale rue Saint-Honoré.

Le Marais

—From Noble Roots to Progressive Urban Village

Just outside the city's historical centre, le Marais ("the swamp") was a favoured residence of the French clergy and nobility, especially after the elegant Place Royale, today's Place des Vosges, was created in 1605. The area's dense medieval streets boast numerous grand *hôtels particuliers*—noble residences—many of which have since been turned into museums. In the 18th century, the aristocracy began to move into the newly developed and more spacious *Faubourg Saint-Germain* on the Left Bank (p42). The void was filled by a vibrant Jewish community, as the Marais became a busy commercial area along the road into central Paris. Fairly run-down by the mid-20th century, efforts were made to revitalise the area, most notably with the modern Centre Pompidou (p29). Its renaissance began in the 1980s when a growing gay presence paved the way for art galleries and fashion boutiques.

Today, the Marais is one of Paris' most upmarket neighbourhoods, yet it has retained many facets that made it popular in the first place. Its southern half, the lively fourth arrondissement—between the Centre Pompidou and the Place des Vosges—boasts the attractions most commonly associated with the Marais: intimate cafés, independent boutiques, Jewish life around the rue des Rosiers, and gay nightlife on and off the rue Sainte-Croix de la Bretonnerie. Across the Seine, the romantic île Saint-Louis meanwhile has largely been untouched by developments in Paris proper. To the north, the quieter third arrondissement and its high street, the rue de Bretagne, though far beyond edgy today, takes in more of the avant-garde character of nearby République (p64). This is also where a small Chinese community has preserved the area's commercial credentials.

LA BASTILLE (PAGE 80)

Rue des Tournelles

Chemin Vert Ⓜ 8

Rue Saint-Gilles

Rue Roger Verlomme

Rue de Béarn

Pl des Vosges

Place des Vosges

hais

Rue Castex

Rue de Lesdiguières

Rue Jacques Cœur

Rue de l'Arsenal

Bd Henry IV

Pavillon de l'Arsenal Ⓜ 4

Rue Saint-Antoine

Le Café Suédois Ⓜ 9

4ème

Rue de Turenne

Rue de Sévigné

Rue Payenne

Rue du Petit Musc

Rue Charles V

Rue des Lions Saint-Paul

Rue Elzevir

lette

Rue Malher

Rue des Rosiers

Saint-Paul Ⓜ 1

Rue Charlemagne

Sully-Morland Ⓜ 7

Rue des Francs Bourgeois

Le Petit Fer à Cheval 14

Rue des Écouffes

Rue du Roi de Sicile

Rue de Fourcy

Quai des Célestins

Quai d'Anjou

Rue Saint-Louis en l'Île

Quai de B.

aux

3 Rooms 1

Rue de Rivoli

Rue François Miron

Rue du Pont Louis-Philippe

Pont Marie Ⓜ 7

Quai de Bourbon

Rue des Deux Ponts

ÎLE SAINT-LOUIS

Rue Saint-Merri

Rue de la Verrerie

Rue de Lobau

Quai de l'Hôtel de Ville

LA SEINE

Rue du .

Hôtel de Ville Ⓜ

Hôtel de Ville

Notre Dame

200 metres

N

Stylish Abode

3 Rooms

1 5 Rue de Moussy
+33 1 44 78 92 00
Ⓜ Hôtel de Ville **1** **11**, Pont Mairie **7**
Apartments from €450/night incl. tax

A boutique hotel venture by couturier Azzedine Alaïa, 3 Rooms blends the charm of its 18th century rue de Moussy surroundings with the fashion world icon's favourite pieces by Arne Jacobsen, Jean Nouvel and Marc Newson. Inspired and co-created by 10 Corso Como and its Milanese 3 Rooms project, the full-floor suites are luxuriously appointed and have private entrances. Alaïa's atelier and flagship store are right next door.

Inside Out Art

Centre Pompidou

2 19 Rue Beaubourg
+33 1 44 78 47 99
centrepompidou.fr
Ⓜ Rambuteau ⑪, Hôtel de Ville ① ⑪
Closed Tue. Open Wed-Mon 11am-9pm

Housed in its 1977 high-tech edifice of exposed colour-coded functional and structural elements, the Centre Pompidou houses the Bibliothèque publique d'information, a vast public library, and the Musée National d'Art Moderne, Europe's largest modern art museum. The centre, locally known as "Beaubourg" after its neighbourhood, received a mixed response at its inauguration but has since been met with "love at second sight".

Sculptor's Atelier

Atelier Brancusi

3 Place Georges-Pompidou
+33 1 44 78 12 33
centrepompidou.fr
Ⓜ Rambuteau ⑪, Hôtel de Ville ① ⑪
Closed Tue. Open Wed-Mon 2pm-6pm

Romanian sculptor Constantin Brancusi spent most of his professional life in Paris. In the first half of the 20th century he created magnificent pieces and mentored talented disciples the likes of Isamu Noguchi at a workshop in the 15th arrondissement. Upon his death, Brancusi bequeathed his entire workshop to the French state, and it was duly reconstructed on the Centre Pompidou's square in 1997. A visit to the atelier offers the visitor the unique experience of gaging an artist's body of work in the setting of its creation.

Architectural Pavilion

Pavillon de l'Arsenal

4 21 Boulevard Morland
+33 1 42 76 33 97
pavillon-arsenal.com
Ⓜ Sully-Morland ⑦, Bastille ① ⑤ ⑧
Closed Mon. Open Tue-Sat 10.30am-6.30pm; Sun 11am-7pm

Located in a relatively nondescript corner between the Marais and the Place de la Bastille (p78), this documentation centre and gallery is a treasure trove for all things related to urban planning and architecture in Paris. The pavilion was built in 1879 for a wood merchant and amateur painter, and was converted to its current use in 1988. Aside from its exhibitions, the Pavillion also publishes reference books and provides a forum for those involved in the city's urban planning. Recent temporary exhibitions covered the Paris of Baron Haussmann and the Olympiades 1970s housing estate.

Art Books

Ofr

5 20 Rue Dupetit-Thouars
+33 1 42 45 72 88
ofrsystem.com
Ⓜ Temple ③, République ③ ⑤ ⑧ ⑪ ⑨
Open daily. Mon-Sat 10am-8pm; Sun
2pm-7pm

Tucked in one of the charming blocks surrounding the square du temple and its picturesque gardens, Ofr is a visual bookshop-cum-gallery offering a stimulating, expertly curated range of art, graphic, design, photography and fashion related publications. The relaxed but edgy vibe beckons the curious *flâneur* lingering outside to enter and discover unique serendipitous finds.

Young Modern People

The Broken Arm

6 12 Rue Perrée
+33 1 44 61 53 60
the-broken-arm.com
Ⓜ Temple ❸, République ❸❺❽⓫❾
Closed Sun/Mon
Boutique: Open Tue-Sat 11am-7pm
Café: Open Tue-Sat 9am-6pm

A particularly well executed concept store and café, The Broken Arm is the brainchild of Guillaume Steinmetz, Anaïs Lafarge and Romain Joste, the founders of fashion and lifestyle website *De jeunes gens modernes*. The aesthetic merges Parisian, Scandinavian and Japanese nuances in a clean lined, modern and welcoming space. The eclectic range of designers featured includes Kenzo and Patrik Ervell. The café's cheerfully tiled floor and generous assortment of indoor plants makes this the perfect spot to brighten up a grey afternoon while enjoying a zesty *orange pressé* and sandwich.

One-Stop Boutique

Merci

7 111 Boulevard Beaumarchais
+33 1 42 77 00 33
merci-merci.com
Ⓜ Saint-Sébastien-Froissart **8**,
Richard-Lenoir **5**
Closed Sun. Open Mon-Sat 10am-7pm

Founded in 2009 by children's clothing creators Bernard and Marie-France Cohen, Merci brings the one-stop fashion, interiors and design boutique concept to the Marais. Aside from offering one of the capital's most stimulating selections of design, Merci stays at the cutting edge by helping to launch the careers of several up-and-coming fashion designers. Après *le shopping*, drop by La Cantine de Merci for a seasonally driven meal.

World Flavours

Marché des Enfants Rouges

8 39 Rue de Bretagne
+33 1 40 11 20 40

Ⓜ Filles du Calvaire **8**, Temple **3**
Closed Mon. Open Tue-Thu 8.30am-1pm, 4pm-7.30pm; Fri/Sat 8.30am-1pm, 4pm-8pm; Sun 8.30am-2pm

A convivial and sophisticated neighbourhood food market, the Marché des Enfants Rouges dishes up artisanal flavours from around the globe. Established in the early 17th century it is reputed to be the oldest covered food market in Paris. The Enfants Rouges was re-vamped in 2000, and its stalls and surrounding shops now offer everything that is required for the wholesome Parisian home-cooked meal, including fresh fruits and vegetables, charcuterie, wine, cheese, oils and spices. For an excellent breakfast in the market, swing by colourfully decorated café *l'estaminet du marché*.

Scandinavian Touch

Le Café Suédois

 11 Rue Payenne
+33 1 44 78 80 11

si.se

Ⓜ Saint-Paul ①, Chemin Vert ⑧

Closed Mon. Open Tue-Sun noon-6pm

Located in a charming *hôtel particulier* housing the Swedish Cultural Institute, Le Café Suédois offers a laid back pocket of Scandinavia in the intellectual and artistic heart of the Marais. After being greeted with a refreshingly non committal "hej", which might come as a shock after the ever present stream of "bonjours" peppering Paris-speak, take your pick of open faced smorgasbord sandwiches vying with fresh cinnamon rolls and banana bread. During the summer months, opt for outdoor seating in the cobble stoned inner courtyard.

Pressed Juices and Futomaki

Bob's Kitchen

10 74 Rue des Gravilliers
+33 9 52 55 11 66

bobsjuicebar.com

Ⓜ Arts et Métiers ❸ ⓫, Réaumur-
Sébastopol ❸ ❹

Open daily. Mon-Fri 8am-3pm; Sat/
Sun 10.30am-4pm

If all that *foie gras* and *calvados* has left you craving some SoCal-style fare, Mark Grossman's hip and healthy Marais institution Bob's Kitchen fits the bill. Bob's whips up everything from Indian stews and fusion *futomaki* to vegan brownies and fresh pressed juices, served to an international crowd of discerning fashionistas on their lunch breaks. Sit at the laid-back communal table and enjoy the surrounding name-dropping induced buzz.

Cuisine et Fantaisie

Derrière

11 69 Rue des Gravilliers
+33 1 44 61 91 95
derriere-resto.com
Ⓜ Arts et Métiers ❸ ⓫, Réaumur-
Sébastopol ❸ ❹
Open daily. Open Mon-Fri noon-
2.30pm, 8pm-11.30pm; Sat 8pm-
11.30pm; Sun noon-4.30pm, 8pm-
11pm

Serial restaurateur *créatif* Mourad
Mazouz of London's Sketch fame
opened his "apartment/restaurant"
Derrière in 2008. Tucked in a
courtyard behind Mazouz' two
other Paris venues, Derrière offers
a stylish home away from home
where guests can indulge in both
cuisine and *fantaisie*. Choose a
seat in the lounge, dining room,
bedroom or boudoir and delve into
such delights as the homemade
terrine of game, roasted cod with
thyme and olive oil or a decadent
dark chocolate mousse.

Bento Meets Brunch

Nanashi

 57 Rue Charlot
+33 1 44 61 45 49
nanashi.fr
Ⓜ Filles du Calvaire ⑧, Temple ③
Open daily. Mon-Sat noon-midnight;
Sun noon-6pm

Nanashi "Le Bento Parisien" is a casual-chic organic take away and restaurant serving *fusion paris-nippone*, as well as some brunchy type outliers to an eco-*bobo* crowd. Drop by on a weekend for the excellent brunch before continuing your culinary adventure at the nearby Marché des Enfants Rouges (p35) and its string of superlative foodie stalls.

Quirky Bistro

Le Taxi Jaune

13 13 Rue Chapon
+33 1 42 76 00 40
Ⓜ Arts et Métiers ❸ ⓫,
Rambuteau ⓫
Closed Sat/Sun. Open Mon-Fri noon-3pm, 8.30pm-10.30pm

An excellent neighbourhood restaurant with a playful décor and laid-back vibe, Le Taxi Jaune is one of the best spots to grab an authentic yet casual meal in the Marais. From perfectly executed *cassolette de moules* to a not-too-sweet *tarte au mirtilles* to be savoured with a strong *café express*, Le Taxi Jaune will uplift spirit and palate no matter the season.

Wine Bar Classic

Le Petit Fer à Cheval

14 30 Rue Vieille du Temple
+33 1 42 72 47 47
cafeine.com
Ⓜ Saint-Paul **1**, Hôtel de Ville **1** **11**
Open daily 9am-2am

In business for over a century, Le Petit Fer à Cheval is a small treasure on the rue Vieille du Temple, one of the Marais' most atmospheric streets. Sit at the bustling horseshoe shaped bar for an invigorating lunch or pop by for an evening *verre de rouge* after exploring the neighbourhood's superlative supply of boutiques. Don't despair if the space appears packed; the bijou-sized bar artfully conceals a dining room in the back.

La Rive Gauche

—Upmarket Intelligentsia

In most riparian cities, the bank opposite from the city proper is distinctly inferior in status. In Paris, *la rive gauche*, the Left Bank, instead became the city's intellectual hub, while the Right Bank specialised in commerce and finance.

The core of the Rive Gauche, the *quartier latin*, is dominated by prestigious universities, notably the Sorbonne and the École des Beaux-Arts (p50). The area's scholarly bent has long fuelled the intellectually charged conversations of the pavement cafés of adjacent Saint-Germain-des-Prés. By the late 18th century, Paris had turned into the intellectual capital of the Western world. The area was site of the 1968 student revolts and home to major post-war intellectual and literary movements, including surrealism and existentialism. Today, Saint-Germain exudes a mix of intellectual flair and an upmarket bourgeois lifestyle, with second hand bookshops sitting alongside international fashion brand boutiques.

Further west along the Boulevard Saint-Germain, the Faubourg Saint-Germain has been the home of the French nobility since the 18th century, when the upper classes moved here from the crowded Marais (p24). After the Revolution, many noble residences, *hôtels particuliers*, were converted into national institutions—the Faubourg Saint-Germain is site of the National Assembly and numerous embassies. In the 19th century, no less than five Universal Exhibitions were held in the area, leaving the Eiffel Tower and today's Musée d'Orsay (p46) in their wake.

Beyond its core, the Left Bank is largely residential. Notable are the *Olympiades*, a 1970s housing development turned Europe's largest Chinatown, and the Butte-aux-Cailles, a quaint urban village.

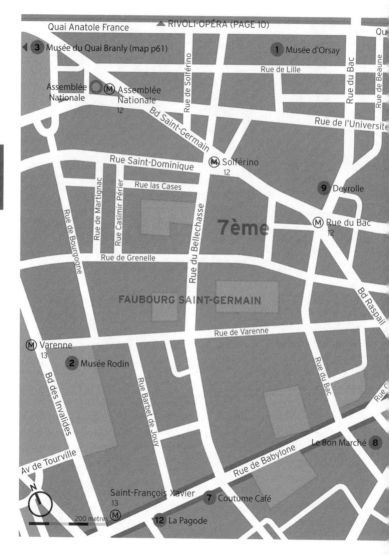

Quai Anatole France
▲ RIVOLI-OPÉRA (PAGE 10)
Qu

◄ 3 Musée du Quai Branly (map p61)

1 Musée d'Orsay

Rue de Lille

Rue de Solférino
Rue du Bac
Rue de Beaune

Assemblée
Nationale
Ⓜ Assemblée
Nationale
12

Bd Saint-Germain

Rue de l'Université

Rue Saint-Dominique
Ⓜ Solférino
12

Rue de Martignac
Rue Casimir Périer
Rue las Cases

9 Deyrolle

Rue de Bourgogne

7ème

Ⓜ Rue du Bac
12

Rue du Bellechasse

Rue de Grenelle

FAUBOURG SAINT-GERMAIN

Bd Raspail

Rue de Varenne

Ⓜ Varenne
13

Rue du Bac

2 Musée Rodin

Rue Barbet de Jouy

Bd des Invalides

Rue

Le Bon Marché 8

Av de Tourville

Rue de Babylone

N

Saint-François Xavier
13
7 Coutume Café

200 metres
Ⓜ
12 La Pagode

▲ RIVOLI-OPÉRA (PAGE 11)

LA SEINE

5 École des Beaux-Arts

Verneuil

6ème

Rue Visconti

11 La Palette

Rue Guénégaud

Rue Dauphine

Rue des Grands Augustins

Rue Jacob

Rue Mazarine

Rue du Pré aux Clercs

Rue des Saints-Pères

Rue Saint-Benoît

Rue de l'Abbaye

Rue de Seine

Rue Saint-André des Arts

QUARTIER
LATIN

Odéon ⓜ
4/10

ⓜ Saint-Germain-des-Prés
4

Bd Saint-Germain

ⓜ Mabillion
10

LA RIVE GAUCHE

Rue des Canettes

Rue Mabillon

Rue M. le Prince

Rue du Four

Rue Bonaparte

Rue Saint-Sulpice

Rue de Tournon

Rue de Condé

Rue de Sèvres

ⓜ St-Sulpice
4

Pl Saint-Sulpice

Rue Garancière

10 Au Bon Saint-Pourçain

Rue de Rennes

Rue Madame

Rue Cassette

6

JARDIN DU
LUXEMBOURG

) Sèvres-Babylone
10/12

Rue du Cherche-Midi

Rue d'Assas

Rue Vaugirard

Rue Guynemer

ⓜ Rennes
12

4 Fondation Cartier

From Railway to Arts Hub

Musée d'Orsay

1 5 Quai Anatole France
+33 1 40 49 48 14
musee-orsay.fr
Ⓜ Solférino ⑫
Closed Mon. Open Tue-Sun 9.30am-6pm; Thu until 9.45pm
Admission €11

Theatrically housed in the former Orsay railway station, built at the height of the Belle Époque for the Universal Exhibition of 1900, le Musée d'Orsay is notable for both its architecture and the magnificent artwork on display. Under threat of being bulldozed and replaced with an office block in 1970, renewed interest in the building's eclectic architecture fortuitously led to the listing of the building. The Musée d'Orsay was inaugurated in 1986 and now houses the world's most stunning collection of western artwork from 1848-1914.

Sculptural Mansion

Musée Rodin

2 79 Rue de Varenne
+33 1 44 18 61 10
musee-rodin.fr
Ⓜ Varenne **13**, La Tour-Maubourg **8**
Closed Mon. Open Tue-Sun 10am-
5.45pm; Wed until 8.45pm
Admission €9

Home to the world's most comprehensive collection of the sculptor's work, le Musée Rodin is housed in L'Hôtel Biron, a glorious *rocaille* style 18th century *hôtel particulier* that was his residence from 1911. Before Rodin made it his home, 20th century glitterati occupying the mansion included Jean Cocteau, Isadora Duncan and Henri Matisse. During the summer months, kick back at the leafy café situated in the museum's sumptuous three-hectare garden.

Where World Cultures Meet

Musée du quai Branly

(3) 37 Quai Branly
+33 1 56 61 70 00
quaibranly.fr
Ⓜ Alma-Marceau ⑨
Closed Mon. Open Tue/Wed/Sun
11am-7pm; Thu-Sat 11am-9pm
Admission €9

The musée du quai Branly houses a treasure trove of indigenous objects and artefacts from Africa, Oceania, Asia and the Americas. Situated in a modern structure designed by Jean Nouvel, the visitor embarks on a stunning visual journey through these geographical regions and their civilisations. The museum's remarkable landscaped garden is the perfect spot for a contemplative afternoon coffee at the crossroads of nature and culture.

Contemporary Art

Fondation Cartier

4 261 Boulevard Raspail
+33 1 42 18 56 50
fondation.cartier.com
Ⓜ Raspail **4** **6**
Closed Mon. Open Tue-Sun 11am-
8pm; Tue until 10pm
Admission €10.50

Situated in an airy glass structure
by Jean Nouvel that offers a perfect
counterpoint to Montparnasse's
19th century apartment blocks
dotting the Boulevard Raspail, the
Fondation Cartier merges corporate
philanthropy with curatorial
dynamism. With a vocation to
expose a wider public to emerging
contemporary artists and to
explore the interstices between
visual art and other forms of artistic
expression, the foundation offers a
refreshingly versatile and creative
iteration of the contemporary
museum.

Premier Art School

École des Beaux-Arts

 14 Rue Bonaparte
+33 1 47 03 50 00

ensba.fr

Ⓜ Saint-Germain-des-Prés ❹, Rue
du Bac ⓬

Opening hours and admission vary
by exhibition, refer to website

With a history of over 350 years, the
École des Beaux-Arts is one of the
world's premier art schools—much
of the work of its *élèves* is exhibited
across the river at the Louvre
museum. Its graduates include
Degas, Delacroix and Monet, but
not Rodin (p47), who failed to be
admitted three times. The school
was the cradle of the eponymous
architectural movement, which
heavily influenced the design
of public building in France and
America. Exhibitions of its students'
work are regularly held in the
glamourous courtyard of its *Palais
des Études* (pictured above).

Tennis by the Senate

Jardin du Luxembourg

 6th Arrondissement
+33 1 40 46 08 88

Ⓜ Notre-Dame-des-Champs ⑫,
Saint-Sulpice ④

Open daily. Opens between 7.30am-
8.15am and closes between 4.30pm-
9.30pm depending on season

The generous garden of the
Luxembourg Palace, today home to
the French Senate, provides a green
escape from the bustle of nearby
Saint-Germain. While inspired by
the Boboli Gardens in Florence,
later additions are in the style of
English and more formal French
gardens. Though a large population
of statues was added beginning in
the late 19th century, the park has
a convivial feel: this is where local
bourgeois families come to play
tennis or remote control model
boats. At dusk, uniformed guards
roam the park to announce its
impending closure for the day.

Aussie Antioxidants

Coutume Café

7 47 Rue de Babylone
+33 1 45 51 50 47
coutumecafe.com
Ⓜ Saint-François-Xavier 13,
Vaneau 10
Closed Mon. Open Tue-Fri 8am-7pm;
Sat/Sun 10am-7pm

Franco-Aussie café and roaster Coutume Café took the Paris brunch scene by storm when it opened in 2011. Located in a posh pocket of the 7ème, a stone's throw from France's first department store, Le Bon Marché (p53), Coutume is the place to go for antioxidant-laden antipodean inspired dishes like organic "detox veggie brunch" accompanied by some of the best coffee in town.

Illustrious Department Store

Le Bon Marché

 24 Rue de Sèvres
+33 1 44 39 80 00
lebonmarche.com
Ⓜ Sèvres-Babylone ⑩ ⑫, Saint-Sulpice ④
Closed Sun. Open Mon-Wed/Sat 10am-8pm; Thu/Fri 10am-9.30pm
La Grande Épicerie: Closed Sun. Open Mon-Sat 8.30am-9pm

Meticulously captured in fiction by Henri de Balzac in his 1883 novel *Au Bonheur des Dames*, Le Bon Marché was France's first department store and maintains its retail élan with the elegance of a *vedette*. Its two radically different halves (one casual, one more formal) are divided between two adjoining buildings, linked by a floating glass walkway. Aside from the superlative fashion element on offer, the La Grande Épicerie grocery department, with its generous *rayon champagne* and cornucopia of exotic fruits, spices and prepared dishes, is worth a trip in of itself.

Artistic Taxidermy

Deyrolle

9 46 Rue du Bac
+33 1 42 22 30 07
deyrolle.fr
Ⓜ Rue du Bac ⑫
Closed Sat/Sun. Open Mon 10am-
1pm, 2pm-7pm; Tue-Fri 10am-7pm

Fancy a stuffed lion? Then Deyrolle is the place to go. A fascinating repository of *taxidermie artistique*, the shop assembles a staggering collection of preserved exotic animals, insects, shells and other natural curiosities. Founded in 1831 by entomologist Emile Deyrolle with a primarily didactic remit, the house branched out during the natural sciences boom, catering to the whimsical tastes of patrons seeking a more stylised, aesthetic expression of taxidermy. Today's Deyrolle is as much gallery as shop, its peppermint green walls highlighting some of the world's most exotic creatures.

Neighbourhood Gem

Au Bon Saint-Pourçain

10 Bis Rue Servandoni
+33 1 43 54 93 63
Ⓜ Saint-Sulpice ④, Mabillon ⑩
Closed Sat/Sun. Open Mon-Fri noon-2.30pm, 7pm-10.30pm

Tucked in one of the small streets behind Saint-Suplice church and its magnificent square, Au Bon Saint-Pourçain transports the diner to the Paris of *le nouveau roman* and Serge Gainsbourg. From the red moleskine banquettes to the tattered bistro-style seating, the small space brims with the conviviality of a local best-kept secret. The simple, delicious, typically Parisian fare is perfectly complemented by the eponymous glass of Saint-Pourçain, a light, acidic and highly food friendly *rouge*.

Art & Champagne

La Palette

11 43 Rue de Seine
+33 1 43 26 68 15
cafelapaletteparis.com
Ⓜ Mabillon ⑩, Saint-Germain-des-
Prés ④
Closed Sun. Open Mon-Sat 8am-2am

The former haunt of Césanne and
Braque remains one of the city's
most uplifting terraces at which
to celebrate art, life and all the
quotidian pleasures over a glass or
two of champagne. Traditionally
the hangout of art students from
the nearby École des Beaux Arts,
the café/restaurant's coveted
Saint-Germain location, at the heart
of Paris' boutique gallery and art
dealer world, makes it one of the
city's more sophisticated A-list
addresses.

Sublime Screen

La Pagode

12 57 Bis Rue de Babylone
+33 1 45 55 48 48
etoile-cinemas.com
Ⓜ Mabillon **10**, Saint-Germain-des-Prés **4**
Screenings daily. Refer to website for showtimes
Tickets €9

A highly original cinema, La Pagode was built in 1896 as a gift from Francois-Emile Morin, the owner of nearby department store Le Bon Marché, to his wife (who soon left him for a colleague). The space's life as the 7th arrondissement's first cinema began in 1931, when the sumptuous Japanese room became the cinephile's screen of choice for catching the latest Bergman, Eisenstein and Cocteau flicks. In the 60s it was famous for screening the New Wave films of Eric Rhomer, Francois Truffaut and Jacques Rozier. Today's Pagode looks rejuvenated and still offers one of the city's best film repertoires.

Passy-Étoile

—West Paris Sophistication and Opulence

Paris' west side and its nearby suburbs are dominated by the Avenues des Champs-Élysées, which links the city's historical centre near the Louvre with the Arc de Triomphe and by extension the La Défense high-rise business district just outside the city limits. The Champs-Élysées and Passy are, along with the Rive Gauche (p42), the wealthiest parts of Paris.

The eighth arrondissement, centred on the Champs-Élysées, is one of Paris' most important business and entertainment hubs, filled with grand cinemas, *haute couture* shops and flashy nightclubs. Popular with tourists, socialites and businessmen alike, the Champs-Élysées and Avenue George V, famously provide a playground for conspicuous consumption. At the same time, the avenue is also the site of the Élysée Palace, home of the French president, and the venue for important military parades.

In contrast, the sixteenth arrondissement, the neighbourhood of Passy could not be more different: residential, bourgeois and very Parisian, it boasts petite parks and boutique museums. The generous 19th century apartment buildings near Passy provide stunning views to the Eiffel Tower and beyond—a view also beheld from the monumental Palais de Chaillot, and the elevated Passy Métro station. On the area's fringes, high society villas are surrounded by lavish landscaped gardens.

On the edge of the city, beyond the bustle of the Champs-Élysées, lies the largely residential seventeenth arrondissement. While its southern fringes are distinctly upmarket, its Batignolles neighbourhood is popular with couples and young families.

M Rue de la Pompe
9
Rue Decamps
Rue des Sablons
PASSY
Rue Scheffer
Av Georges Mandel
Rue Greuze
Av de l'Eylau
Rue Longchamp
Rue Raymond Poincaré
Rue Saint-Didier
16ème
◀ 2 Fondation Le Corbusier
Av Paul Doumer
Pl du Trocadéro
M Trocadéro
6/9
Rue Vineuse
Rue Longchamp
Av du Président Wilson
Rue Benjamin Franklin
Palais de Chaillot
TROCADÉRO
Av Albert de Mun
Av de l'Iéna
Bd Delessert
Rue Fresne
M Passy
6
Av de New York
Pont de l'Iéna
LA SEINE
N
200 metres
Quai Branly
7ème
Eiffel Tower
Musée du

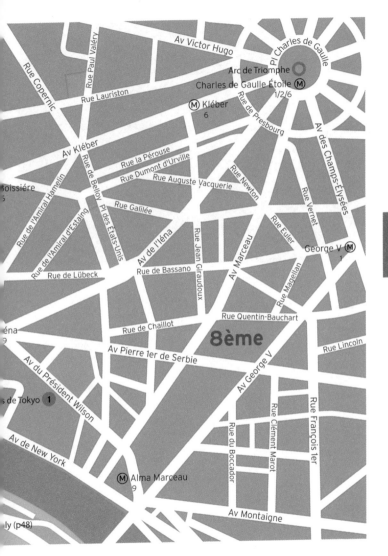

Monumentalist Palace

Palais de Tokyo

① 13 Avenue du Président Wilson
+33 1 49 52 02 04

palaisdetokyo.com

Ⓜ léna ⑨

Closed Tue. Mon Wed-Mon noon-
midnight

Inaugurated in 1937 for the
International Exhibition of Arts
and Technology, the hefty
monumentalist structure housing
the Palais de Tokyo hangs over the
Trocadéro gardens with theatrical
aplomb. Revamped and revitalised
in 2002, the Palais now produces
creative exhibitions focusing on
emerging work from the French
and international contemporary
art scenes. With its lofty ceilings
and whimsical atmosphere, fusion
restaurant Tokyo Eat is an inspiring
spot for lunch.

Iconic Architecture

Fondation
Le Corbusier

 8-10 Square du Docteur Blanche

+33 1 42 88 41 53

fondationlecorbusier.fr

Ⓜ Jasmin ⑨

Maison La Roche: Closed Sun. Open Mon 1.30pm-6pm; Tue-Sat 10am-6pm

Maison Jeanneret: Closed Sat/Sun. Open Mon 1.30pm-6pm; Tue-Thu 10am-12.30pm, 1.30pm-6pm; Fri 10am-12.30pm, 1.30pm-5pm

Guided tours available. Refer to website for details

Established in 1968, the Fondation Le Corbusier is located in the La Roche-Jeanneret House, designed by the architect in 1923-1925. The iconic structure, with its flat roof and white stucco walls, was Le Corbusier's third commission, built for the wealthy bachelor Monsieur La Roche. The Maison Roche houses the world's largest collection of Le Corbusier drawings, studies and plans (more than 8,000), as well as 450 of the architect's paintings and his photographic archives. The 16th arrondissements was popular with the pre-war architectural avant-garde and Le Corbusier's home from 1933 to 1965.

St-Denis-République
—Socialist, Diverse and Cutting Edge

Paris' east side, downwind from the city centre, was historically the home of the working classes and the source of labour movements. The area's leftist credentials are epitomised by its focal point, the Place de la République with its colossal statue of Marianne, the symbol of the French state, holding a tablet inscribed with the Rights of Man.

After Paris' decline as a manufacturing hub, the area became neglected, turning into a destination for new immigrants—a third of its residents are now foreign-born. The Faubourg Saint-Denis in the tenth arrondissement also acquired a reputation for crime and prostitution. Discovered by the creative set priced out of the Marais (p24), Saint-Denis, République and Oberkampf have become a melting pot where working class old timers and recent immigrants mingle with hipsters and *bobo* types.

A particular attraction of the area is the Canal Saint-Martin. Linking the city's northeast with the River Seine, the canal played an important role in the area's industrialisation in the 19th century. Its banks are now one of the most happening parts of Paris, attracting artists and creative types to its countless small shops and cafés. Visually set apart from a city more commonly associated with grand boulevards, the canal also exudes a degree of calm and space that is usually absent in dense Paris.

The Parc de la Villette, on the edge of Paris proper and the *périphérique* ring motorway, was formerly the site of Paris' slaughterhouses. Its green spaces are now home to the Cité de la Musique and the Paris conservatory.

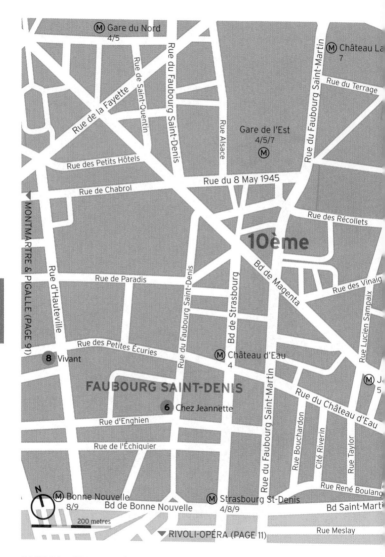

Ⓜ Gare du Nord
4/5

Ⓜ Château La
7

Rue du Terrage

Rue de la Fayette

Rue de Saint-Quentin

Rue du Faubourg Saint-Denis

Rue Alsace

Gare de l'Est
4/5/7
Ⓜ

Rue du Faubourg Saint-Martin

Rue des Petits Hôtels

Rue du 8 May 1945

Rue de Chabrol

Rue des Récollets

10ème

Rue de Paradis

Bd de Magenta

Rue des Vinaig

Rue d'Hauteville

Rue du Faubourg Saint-Denis

Bd de Strasbourg

Rue Lucien Sampaix

Rue des Petites Écuries

Ⓜ Château d'Eau
4

8 Vivant

FAUBOURG SAINT-DENIS

Rue du Faubourg Saint-Martin

Rue du Château d'Eau

Ⓜ J
5

6 Chez Jeannette

Rue d'Enghien

Rue Bouchardon

Cité Riverin

Rue Taylor

Rue de l'Échiquier

Rue René Boulang

Ⓜ Bonne Nouvelle
8/9

N

Bd de Bonne Nouvelle

Ⓜ Strasbourg St-Denis
4/8/9

Bd Saint-Mart

200 metres

▼ RIVOLI-OPÉRA (PAGE 11)

Rue Meslay

◄ MONTMARTRE & PIGALLE (PAGE 91)

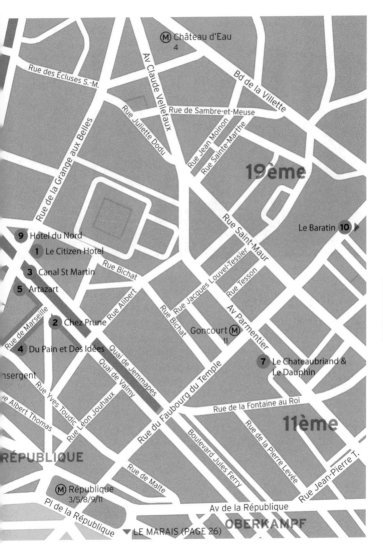

(M) Château d'Eau
4

Rue des Écluses S.-M.

Av Claude Vellefaux

Bd de la Villette

Rue Juliette Dodu

Rue de Sambre-et-Meuse

Rue Jean Moinon

Rue Sainte-Marthe

19ème

Rue de la Grange aux Belles

Rue Saint-Maur

Le Baratin 10 ▶

9 Hotel du Nord

1 Le Citizen Hotel

Rue Bichat

3 Canal St Martin

5 Artazart

Rue Alibert

Rue Jacques Louvel-Tessier

Rue Tesson

Rue de Marseille

2 Chez Prune

Rue Bichat

Av Parmentier

4 Du Pain et Des Idées

Quai de Jemmapes

Goncourt (M)
11

Quai de Valmy

7 Le Chateaubriand &
Le Dauphin

insergent

Rue Yves Toudic

Rue Léon Jouhaux

Rue du Faubourg du Temple

Rue de la Fontaine au Roi

e Albert Thomas

11ème

Rue de la Pierre Levée

Boulevard Jules Ferry

Rue Jean-Pierre T.

RÉPUBLIQUE

Rue de Malte

(M) République
3/5/8/9/11

Pl de la République

Av de la République

OBERKAMPF

▼ LE MARAIS (PAGE 26)

Canal-side Hotel

Le Citizen Hotel

1 96 Quai de Jemmapes
+33 1 83 62 55 50
lecitizenhotel.com
Ⓜ Jacques Bonsergent **5**,
Gare de l'Est **4** **5** **7**
Doubles from €189/night incl. tax

Comfy and eco-chic, Le Citizen Hotel brings relaxed flair to the Canal Saint-Martin. Located in the midst of the Canal's *bobo-artistique* restaurants, cafés and boutiques, the hotel's setting is unbeatable. Rooms are sunny, many with picturesque views of the canal, and breakfast is always included. This is a great option if you're looking to explore some of the right bank's edgier pockets, and if you're popping over to London or Germany by train, the Gare de l'Est and Gare du Nord are conveniently close by.

Brunch with Friends

Chez Prune

2 36 Rue Beaurepaire
+33 1 42 41 30 47

Ⓜ Jacques Bonsergent ⑤,
République ③ ⑤ ⑧ ⑨ ⑪

Open daily. Mon-Sat 8am-2am; Sun
10am-2am

Chez Prune's convivial atmosphere and prime placement on the banks of the Canal Saint-Martin contribute to its status as a *bobo* classic. Sit along the wooden banquette and delve into a plate of charcuterie with a glass of wine and some good company. Prune pulls off Sunday brunch with panache, spinning off smoked salmon plates, scrambled eggs and fresh pressed juices to the delight of its faithful patrons. After brunch, check out the fabulous selection of design related books at neighbouring Artazart (p72).

Canal Life

Canal Saint-Martin

3 10th Arrondissement
Ⓜ Jacques Bonsergent Ⓢ,
Gare de l'Est ④⑤⑦

Public access

Interspersed with picturesque cafés, wine bars and boutiques, a stroll along the charming Canal Saint-Martin surely ranks among the city's greatest pleasures. Funded by a wine tax levied by Napoleon I in 1802, the building of the canal linking the Ourcq and Seine rivers was intended to supply the burgeoning city with a sanitary supply of fresh water while easing the flow of goods into the heart of the metropolis. Today, the canal plays a photogenic role in the revitalization of the ebullient 10th arrondissement.

The Best Baguette

Du Pain et Des Idées

④ 34 Rue Yves Toudic
+33 1 42 40 44 52
dupainetdesidees.com
Ⓜ Jacques Bonsergent ⑤,
République ③⑤⑧⑨⑪
Closed Sat/Sun. Open Mon-Fri
6.45am-8pm

Fashion world veteran turned bread expert Christophe Vasseur stumbled upon an attractive but failing *boulangerie* near the Canal Saint-Martin in the early 2000's. It wasn't long before his fresh and natural loaves populated Du Pain et Des Idées' flour-dusted shelves. By 2010, the bakery had been crowned best in Paris by Gault and Millau. So whether you're seeking le pain des amis, or a more exotic invention like the *croissant au thé matcha*, a stopover at Du Pain et Des Idées is an absolute must.

Premier Visual Bookshop

Artazart

5 83 Quai de Valmy
+33 1 40 40 24 00
artazart.com

Ⓜ Jacques Bonsergent **5**,
Gare de l'Est **4 5 7**

Open daily. Mon-Fri 10.30am-7.30pm;
Sat 11am-7.30pm; Sun 2pm-8pm

Artazart launched as a graphic design related website in 1999. The web version of the present-day shop allowed *internautes* the luxury of flicking through the latest design-centric pages long before the practice became mainstream. Today's Artazart is one of the city's premier visual bookshops, offering a stunning selection of graphic, typographic, photographic and art historical gems on the charming banks of the Canal Saint-Martin (p70). An exhibition room affords the browser the luxury of building the bridge between theory and practice.

Revamped Classic

Chez Jeannette

6 47 Rue du Faubourg Saint-Denis

+33 1 47 70 30 89

chezjeannette.com

Ⓜ Château d'Eau **4**, Strasbourg-Saint-Denis **4** **8** **9**

Open daily. Mon-Sat 8am-2am; Sun 9am-2am

One of the pioneers of Saint-Denis' ascension to hipdom, Chez Jeannette, a revamped *Faubourg* institution, is a rock star of a watering hole. Most of the 1940s décor has been restored by the bar's new owners, giving the space a playful and authentic retro vibe. Music at peak decibels, a *tendance*-driven crowd and the cheap beer on tap make this one of the right bank's most playfully endearing spots.

Brilliant Gastronomy

Le Chateaubriand & Le Dauphin

7 129 Avenue Parmentier
+33 1 43 57 45 95

lechateaubriand.net

Ⓜ Goncourt ⑪, Parmentier ③

Le Chateaubriand: Closed Sun/Mon. Open Tue-Sat from 7.30pm with reservation, from 9.30pm without reservation

Le Dauphin: Closed Sun/Mon. Open Tue-Sat with reservation from noon-1.30pm, 7.30pm-8.30pm

A brilliant *néo-bistrot*, Le Chateaubriand's Basque chef Iñaki Aizpitarte artfully fuses Gallic fare with Asian and South American accents. The décor is modern bistro-chic and its popularity and reputation translates into a perpetual buzz. The 50-euro tasting menu delights the palate and landed Le Chateaubriand firmly in 18th place on Restaurant Magazine's Diners Club Academy list of the world's top 50 restaurants. Le Dauphin (pictured above) is Le Chateaubriand's casual little brother. Here the focus is on innovative tapas, served in a mirrors and Cararra marble setting.

Sumptuous Cuisine

Vivant

8 43 Rue des Petites Écuries
+33 1 42 46 43 55
vivantparis.com
Ⓜ Poissonnière **7**,
Bonne Nouvelle **8 9**
Vivant Table: Closed Sat/Sun.
Open Mon-Fri for lunch and dinner
(reservation only)
Vivant Cave: Closed Sat/Sun. Open
Mon-Fri 5pm-midnight

Pierre Jancou's fabulous restaurant, Vivant Table, and culinary wine bar, Vivant Cave, reflect the innovative spirit of a *quartier* in transformation. From the artfully sourced regional produce and biodynamic wines to the sumptuous coffee beans by a small Veronese *torréfacteur*, this is *cuisine* at its best. While chefs Atsumi Souta (Table) and Yamamoto Masaaki (Cave) whip up a gastronomic storm, admire the Gilardoni-style faïences depicting exquisite birds reflecting the space's origins as a 1903 bird shop.

Northern Delight

Hotel du Nord

9 102 Quai de Jemmapes
+33 1 40 40 78 78
hoteldunord.org

Ⓜ Jacques Bonsergent **5**,
Gare de l'Est **4 5 7**

Open daily
Café: 9am-1.30pm
Restaurant: noon-3pm, 8pm-
midnight

Immortalised in Marcel Carné's
1930s film "Hotel du Nord", this late
19th century stalwart of the blue
collar *"faubourgs de l'Est"* has been
restored and revitalised, taking its
present shape as a seductive café/
restaurant. During the summer
months, canal-side chairs and
tables spring up as the perfect
setting for a glass of rosé, while
brisker weather pairs perfectly with
the space's plush and cosy interior,
complete with chess boards and a
library.

Hilltop Home Cooking

Le Baratin

⑩ 3 Rue Jouye-Rouve
+33 1 43 49 39 70
Ⓜ Pyrénées ⑪, Belleville ❷⑪
Closed Sun/Mon. Open Tue-Fri
12.15pm-2pm, 7.30pm-11pm; Sat
7.30pm-11pm

Le Baratin sits on a precipice in the heights of blue-collar Belleville, overhanging the Paris sprawl. Its hearty bistro menu, natural wines, friendly but rough-around-the-edges disposition and bare bones but atmospheric décor make it an absolute winner for a simple meal. Well worth the trek up the hill for the old school bistro experience alone, a post-gastronomic walk around the climes of Belleville opens the window to an intriguing and less explored dimension of the city.

La Bastille

—Boisterous Nightlife and Delightful Gastronomy

With its anarchistic roots, the Bastille neighbourhood has maintained a rough-around-the-edges feel, interspersed with calm residential pockets and some hidden culinary gems. The area derives its name from the circular Place de la Bastille, where the French Revolution began in 1789 with the storming of the Bastille prison—though the July Column at its centre commemorates the second insurrection of 1830.

The Place de La Bastille is now a centre of youthful Paris nightlife, and also home to the Opéra de la Bastille, a post-modernist edifice inaugurated in 1989. Just a few blocks east of the hustle-and-bustle of the Bastille square begins the vast grid of grand avenues and generous apartment buildings that make up one of Europe's most densely populated residential areas. The twelfth arrondissement is dotted with beautiful garden squares lined by pavement cafés and innovative restaurants.

The nearby Gare de Lyon station, with its famous Train Bleu restaurant of 1901, is one of the city's main gateways to the south and east, including direct connections to fashionable resorts of the *Côte d'Azur*. On the neighbourhood's far fringes, beyond the *périphérique* motorway, lies the Bois de Vincennes, a pleasantly shrubby parkland by the standards of Paris' otherwise painstakingly manicured green spaces.

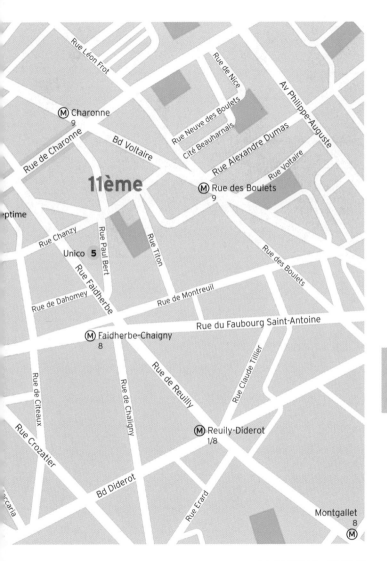

Rue Léon Frot

Rue de Nice

Rue de Charonne

Rue Alexandre Dumas

Av Philippe-Auguste

Ⓜ Charonne
9

Bd Voltaire

Rue Neuve des Boulets

Cité Beauharnais

Rue Voltaire

11ème

Ⓜ Rue des Boulets
9

ptime

Rue Chanzy

Rue Paul Bert

Rue Titon

Rue des Boulets

Unico 5

Rue Faidherbe

Rue de Dahomey

Rue de Montreuil

Rue du Faubourg Saint-Antoine

Ⓜ Faidherbe-Chaigny
8

Rue de Citeaux

Rue de Chaligny

Rue de Reuilly

Rue Claude Tillier

Rue Crozatier

Ⓜ Reuily-Diderot
1/8

ceria

Bd Diderot

Rue Erard

Montgallet
8
Ⓜ

Painterly Bistro

Le Bistrot du Peintre

1 116 Avenue Ledru Rollin
+33 1 47 00 34 39
bistrotdupeintre.com
Ⓜ Ledru-Rollin 8, Voltaire 9
Open daily 7am-2am

On a bustling corner of café-dotted Boulevard Ledru-Rollin, Le Bistrot du Peintre's curvy Belle Époque features, cheerful vibe and quality bistro fare make it a standout. In business since 1902, the bistro excels at the menu du jour "formule" as well as serving the gastronomic and oenological needs of characters from all walks of life, including *flâneurs*, fashionistas and poets alike.

Belle Époque Splendour

Le Square Trousseau

2 1 Rue Antoine Vollon
+33 1 43 43 06 00
squaretrousseau.com
Ⓜ Ledru-Rollin **⑧**
Open daily 8am-2am

Le Square Trousseau sits elegantly on its eponymous *place*, one of the city's most charming, with tables spilling out onto the pavement under a majestic awning. The café's Belle Époque interior, complete with tulip light fittings and gold plated mouldings, have landed it a supporting role in many a French film. During the summer, sit at the terrace with a *café* and the press of the day. In colder months, cosy up indoors with a glass of perfectly spiced mulled wine.

Italian Chic

Vilia

③ 26 Rue de Cotte
+33 9 80 44 20 15
viliavilia.com
Ⓜ Ledru-Rollin ⑧
Closed Wed. Open Tue/Thu/Fri 6pm-11pm. Sat-Mon 11am-3pm, 6pm-11pm

Occupying what was once a furrier's quarters, Vilia's atmospheric décor à la Sophia Loren, complete with 1950s pieces and dusky boiseries, combined with sumptuous Italian fare, make it the ultimate stylish but friendly neighbourhood bistro. From the poached cod on a bed of bright violet *vitelotte* potatos, to the panna cotta with hibiscus, you will not be disappointed.

Tantalising Fare

Septime

4 80 Rue de Charonne
+33 1 43 67 38 29
septime-charonne.fr
Ⓜ Faidherbe-Chaligny 8,
Charonne 9
Closed Sat/Sun. Open Mon-Fri
7.30pm-10pm; Tue-Fri 12.30pm-2pm,
7.30pm-10pm

An excellent, unpretentious restaurant that has made its mark on the city's culinary scene, Septime's head chef Bertrand Grébaut creatively underscores French classics with Asian accents. Septime's location at the epicentre of the Bastille's belt of happening eateries, as well as its place on the Diners Club Academy list of the world's 50 best restaurants, ensure that the candle lit space is perpetually filled to the brim.

Steak and Malbec

Unico

5 15 Rue Paul Bert
+33 1 43 67 68 08
resto-unico.com
Ⓜ Faidherbe-Chaligny **8**,
Rue des Boulets **9**
Closed Sun. Open Mon 8pm-
10.45pm; Tue-Sat 12.15pm-2pm, 8pm-
10.45pm (Fri/Sat until 11pm)

Like any Argentine worth his salt, Unico does steak in a big way. Mouth-wateringly juicy, seductively garnished with *chimichurri* sauce, or practically *bleu*, each rendition is executed with precision and aplomb. And what better way to embolden your *bife de chorizo con patatas al horno* than with a nice round glass of brambly Malbec? The space's mock 70s décor is orange, over the top, and fabulous.

Montmartre & Pigalle

—Hillside Bohemia and Red Lights

The hill of Montmartre, the highest elevation in Paris, is famous for the white-domed Sacré Cœur Basilica at its summit and the Pigalle red-light district below. Its quaint winding streets and gas-lamp lit stairs have inspired many a visitor to take root in this city.

Historically located outside city limits, the area soon developed a freewheeling character. Montmartre has also played an important role in the visual arts and many important artists, among them Dalí, Modigliani, Monet, Mondrian, Picasso and van Gogh, have lived or worked on its cobblestoned streets. In contrast to this liberal backdrop, the Roman Catholic Sacré Cœur Basilica, was inspired by France's defeat against Prussia in 1870, which the Church attributed to the apparent moral decline since the French Revolution. Though incredibly touristy today, especially around the Sacré Cœur and the nearby Place du Tertre, Montmartre has retained its bohemian character and its streets continue to be home to many artists.

At the foot of its hill, Montmartre meets the city's Haussmanian street grid and the seedy nightlife and red-light district of Pigalle. Dotted with revue bars and cabarets, some of its glamorous names like the Moulin Rouge date back to the Belle Époque. Just steps away, the residential neighbourhood of Saint-Georges, or "South Pigalle", has become a preferred haunt for creative professionals and boasts everything from yoga studios to a growing number of interesting restaurants and speciality retail outlets.

Squeezed between Montmartre and the rail tracks of the Gare du Nord are the immigrant neighbourhoods of La Goutte d'Or and La Chapelle. Besides boasting ethnic restaurants from every corner of the world, the area is a draw for its textile trade and the famously cheap Tati department store.

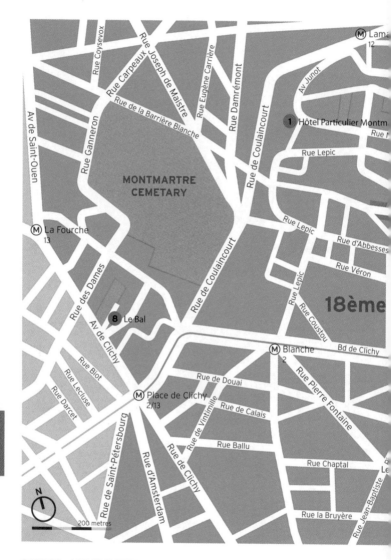

M Lama
12

Rue Coysevox
Rue Carpeaux
Rue Joseph de Maistre
Rue de la Barrière Blanche
Rue Eugène Carrière
Rue Damrémont
Av Junot

Av de Saint-Ouen

Rue Ganneron

Rue de Coulaincourt

1 Hôtel Particulier Montm

Rue I

Rue Lepic

**MONTMARTRE
CEMETARY**

Rue Lepic

Rue d'Abbesses

M La Fourche
13

Rue Véron

Rue des Dames

Rue de Coulaincourt

Rue Lepic

18ème

Rue Coustou

Av de Clichy

8 Le Bal

Bd de Clichy

M Blanche
2

Rue Biot

Rue de Douai

Rue Pierre Fontaine

Rue Lecluse

Rue Darcet

M Place de Clichy
2/13

Rue de Vintimille
Rue de Calais

Rue de Saint-Pétersbourg

Rue Ballu

Rue d'Amsterdam

Rue de Clichy

Rue Chaptal

Le

Rue la Bruyère

Rue Jean-Baptiste

N

200 metres

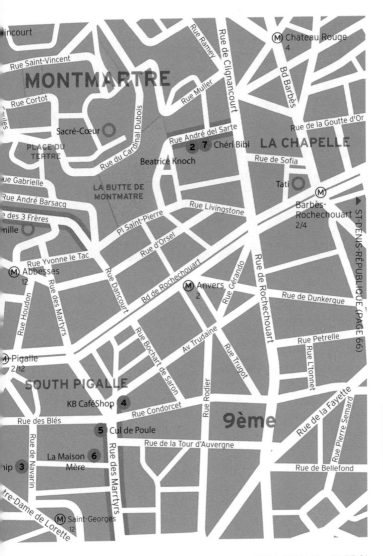

MONTMARTRE (title on map)

Rue Saint-Vincent
Rue Cortot
Sacré-Cœur
PLACE DU TERTRE
Rue Gabrielle
LA BUTTE DE MONTMARTRE
Rue André Barsacq
des 3 Frères
mille
Rue Yvonne le Tac
M Abbesses
12
Rue Houdon
Rue des Martyrs
M) Pigalle
2/12
SOUTH PIGALLE
KB CaféShop **4**
Rue des Blés
5 Cul de Poule
La Maison **6**
Mère
hip **3**
Rue de Navarin
Notre-Dame de Lorette
M Saint-Georges
12

ncourt
Rue Ramey
Rue de Clignancourt
M Chateau Rouge
4
Bd Barbès
Rue Muller
Rue du Cardinal Dubois
Rue André del Sarte
2 7 Chéri Bibi
Beatrice Knoch
Rue de la Goutte d'Or
LA CHAPELLE
Rue de Sofia
Tati
M
Barbès-Rochechouart
2/4
Rue Livingstone
Pl Saint-Pierre
Rue d'Orsel
Rue Dancourt
Bd de Rochechouart
M Anvers
2
Rue Gérando
Rue de Rochechouart
Rue de Dunkerque
Av Trudaine
Rue Bochart de Saron
Rue Truget
Rue Petrelle
Rue L'Etonnet
Rue Condorcet
Rue Rodier
9ème
Rue de la Tour d'Auvergne
Rue de la Fayette
Rue Pierre Semard
Rue de Bellefond
ST-DENIS-RÉPUBLIQUE (PAGE 66)

Exclusive Heights

Hôtel Particulier Montmartre

1 23 Avenue Junot
+33 1 53 41 81 40
hotel-particulier-montmartre.com
Ⓜ Lamarck-Caulaincourt 12
Suites from €390/night incl. tax

Housed in an elegant mansion hidden within a private cobblestoned courtyard in the more exclusive fringes of Montmartre, Hôtel Particulier Montmartre's five suites marry opulent glamour with quirky *je ne sais quoi*. The house was once owned by the Hermès family and maintains the feel of an opulent personal residence. Enjoy breakfast in the Louis Benech landscaped garden or an aperitif in the luxuriously garbed salon before heading out for a night on the town.

Subtle Gems

Beatrice Knoch

2 17 Rue André del Sarte
+33 1 42 57 97 09

Ⓜ Château Rouge ❹, Anvers ❷
Closed Mon/Wed/Sun. Open Tue/
Thu-Sat 11am-7pm

In a charming, cobble stoned *coin* of Paris' most romantic neighbourhood, Beatrice Knoch's magnificently subtle jewels add lustre to their shabby-chic setting. Based in Paris for most of the last decade, German-born Beatrice melds the Teutonic obsession with high quality materials with Parisian refinement and creativity. A browse through the boutique/atelier and its string of perfectly formed pieces will surely lead to a purchase or two…

South Pigalle Must Haves

Le Rocketship

3 13 Bis Rue Henry Monnier
   +33 1 48 78 23 66
lerocketship.com
Ⓜ Saint-Georges ⑫, Pigalle ➁ ⑫
Closed Sun/Mon. Open Tue-Sat 11am-
7.30pm

Le Rocketship is an attractive boutique/café in the heart of trendy "SoPi". Owner Benoît Touche sources must-have *objets* from across the globe, artfully assembling them to the delight of the denizens of the 9ème. Grab a cappuccino and jot down some notes with one of the shop's range of stylish Midori pens, or browse the shelves to discover splendidly washed out Fog Linen kitchen cloths, Dylan Design Company's artisinally crafted Rocketship shaped lamp or Les Toiles Blanche's Eiffel Tower cushion, just to name a few.

Contemporary Café

KB CaféShop

4 53 Avenue Trudaine
+33 1 56 92 12 41

Ⓜ Pigalle ❷ ⓬

Open daily. Open Mon-Fri 7.30am-
6.30pm; Sat/Sun 9am-6.30pm

South Pigalle's go-to spot for excellent espresso based drinks, freshly squeezed juices, smoothies, salads, cakes and other contemporary café classics, KB Café Shop affirms the neighbourhood's position as an international boho hotbed. Sip your flat white in the attractive interior or take your long black for a trot down the boutique dotted Rue des Martyrs.

SoPi Dining

Cul de Poule

5 53 Rue des Martyrs
+33 1 53 16 13 07

Ⓜ Pigalle ❷ ⓫

Closed Sun. Open Mon-Sat noon-2.30pm, 8pm-11.30pm

An excellent casual eatery on the trendy Rue des Martyrs, Cul de Poule dishes out a fabulous menu to the inhabitants of SoPi. At once neighbourhood *résto* and backdrop for the creative scene, complete with Shoboshobo mural and giant pillows, Cul de Poule is a restaurant with a personality. The outdoor terrace overlooking the picturesque streetscape is not to be missed in summer.

Le Franco-Americain

La Maison Mère

6   4 Rue de Navarin
+33 1 42 81 11 00
lamaisonmere.fr
Ⓜ Saint-Georges ⑫, Pigalle ❷ ⑫
Open daily. Mon-Sat noon-3pm, 7pm-2am; Sun noon-4pm

This South Williamsburg-meets-South Pigalle brasserie whips up refined Franco-American concoctions in a jovial setting. Subway tiles merge seamlessly with classic bistro chairs and all aspects, from the staff to the music, are at once happening and relaxed. Enjoy a warm summer's day out on the terrace overlooking the neighbourhood's characteristically charming architecture, while rubbing shoulders with the hood's espresso sipping *bobos*.

Effervescent Meal

Chéri Bibi

7 15 Rue André del Sarte
+33 1 42 54 88 96
Ⓜ Château Rouge ❹, Anvers ❷
Closed Sun. Open Mon-Sat 6pm-2am

With its playful retro furniture and delectable home-cuisine, Chéri Bibi is a delight. Mingle with the local artists and intellectuals dropping by for their evening *apéro* at the bar before hitting the two or three-course menu. For a more intimate experience, check out Chéri Bibi's cosy sister restaurant La Famille on the opposite side of the hill.

Visual Stimulation

Le Bal

8 6 Impasse de la Défense
+33 1 44 70 75 51
le-bal.fr
Ⓜ Place de Clichy ❷ ⓫,
La Fourche ⓫
Gallery: Closed Mon/Tue. Open Wed/
Fri noon-8pm; Thu noon-10pm; Sat
11am-8pm; Sun 11am-7pm
Café: Closed Mon. Open Tue-Sat
noon-8pm; Sun 11am-7pm
Admission €5

Occupying a former 1920s dance
hall, Le Bal is a cutting-edge
venue dedicated to the image-
document in all its forms and to
the exploration of the genre's role
in representing reality. Started
in 2008, the project curates
fascinating exhibitions focusing on
photography, video, film and new
media. Architects Agence Search's
transformation of the original
space into a free-flowing gallery
and attractive garden-side café and
bookshop make a visit to Le Bal
particularly pleasing.

Essentials

Airport Transfer

Paris is served by two major airports: Charles de Gaulle (also known as "Roissy"), which opened in 1975, and the smaller Orly, previously the city's main airport. At both airports, taxis are usually available at Arrivals.

Charles de Gaulle (CDG): The airport lies 25km northeast of Paris in the city's relatively unprosperous northern periphery. A taxi to the centre takes about 45 minutes and costs €35-40. By rail, the airport is connected by the RER B commuter train. The service runs 8 times per hour (4 of which run directly to central Paris) and takes 30-35 minutes to Gare du Nord (single ticket, €9.50). There are also two bus services, "Roissybus" (to Opéra, €10) and "Les Cars Air France" (with stops across the city, €17). The bus journey is longer (up to 1h) but tends to be more pleasant than taking the RER.

Orly (ORY): Orly lies 15km south of Paris and is easily accessible by taxi. A ride to the centre takes about 30 minutes and will cost €25-30. The airport is connected to RER B commuter train services at Antony (via Orlyval lightrail, 40 mins, €11.30), though a quicker and less cumbersome alternative is the bus service operated by "Orlybus" (to Denfert-Rochereau, €7.20) and "Les Cars Air France" (with stops across the city, €12).

Taxis

Paris taxis are affordable but highly regulated and sparse. The queues at the Gare du Nord taxi stand are notorious and taxis are often simply unavailable: when it rains, during rush hour, after concerts, or at any time one would conceivably want to use a taxi.

That said, taxis can be booked in advance or for immediate use. The major operators are Taxis Bleus (taxis-bleus.com, +33 8 91 70 10 10) and Taxis G7 (taxisg7.fr, +33 1 47 39 47 39). Advance bookings incur a €5 charge in addition to the fare. Note that booked taxis start the meter from the moment they leave to pick you up, and may not let you know that they have arrived at the appointed pick up. Taxis typically refuse to pick up passengers if a taxi stand is nearby.

Once settled behind the clock and at good terms with the driver, Paris taxis are a fairly smooth way to get around the city. A cross-town trip form Gare du Nord to Passy will take 25 minutes and should not cost more than €15. The larger taxi companies usually accept credit cards for higher fares.

Public Transport
The Paris Métro is the archetype urban railway and has lent its name to "metro" systems all over the world. Its network is very dense with short distances between stations. The sizes of its cars and tunnels were deliberately chosen to prevent suburban and national trains from running into and across the city.

The Métro operates from 5.30am to 12.40am, except for Friday and Saturday nights when the service ends at 1.40am. Frequencies between trains are low as 2 minutes during rush hour and up to 8-10 minutes during off hours and on Sundays. Some lines, including numbers 1, 12 and 14 have a more family friendly feel than others, especially at night.

A single ticket costs €1.70 and is also valid on buses, trams and RER commuter trains within city limits. A carnet of ten tickets costs €12.70. Weekly passes (€19.80) are available on Navigo pass smart cards; note that their validity always starts on a Monday! There are also "ParisVisite" day passes (€10.55-€33.70) valid for any 1, 2, 3 or 5 consecutive days.

Tipping
Tipping is not a comprehensive part of French social life. By law a 15% service charge is included in any restaurant price. Tips do exist but are only expected for good or attentive service. In cafés round up, in taxis and restaurants add up to 5% for good service. Save the maximum 10% for the day you receive very good service at a top-notch establishment.

Safety
Paris is a rich city and the French state highly redistributive, but Paris and its suburbs have extreme wealth disparities. On a macro level, the city's southwest has historically been bourgeois and its northeast relatively deprived and more prone to crime. Paris is quite densely populated, leaving only smaller streets deserted at night.

Index

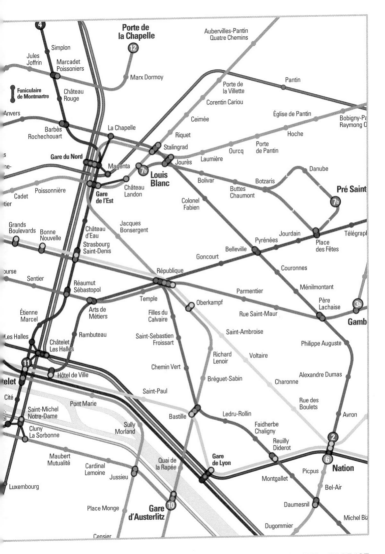

Credits

Published by Analogue Media, LLC
244 5th Avenue, Suite 2446, New York, NY 10001, United States

Edited by Alana Stone
Layout & Production by Stefan Horn

For more information about the Analogue Guides series, or to find out about availability and purchase information, please visit analogueguides.com

First Edition 2014
ISBN: 978-0-9838585-5-3

Typefaces: Neutraface 2, Myriad Pro and Interstate
Paper: Munken Lynx

Printed in Barcelona by Agpograf, S.A.

Analogue Media would like to thank all contributing venues, designers, manufacturers, agencies and photographers for their kind permission to reproduce their work in this book.

Cover design by Dustin Wallace
Proofread by John Leisure
Metro Map courtesy of www.london-tubemap.com © Mark Noad

All photography credited to the listed venues unless stated otherwise:

Rivoli-Opéra (9) Stefan Horn (12/13) Paul Boywer (14) Luc Boegly (15) Paul Bowyer (17) Gilles Ronin (18) Jacky Corbel (21) Djamel Dine-Zitout (22) Paul Bowyer

Le Marais (25) Ron Gunzburger (28) Christoph Kicherer (30) Lauren Barr (31) © Antoine Espinasseau (32) Paul Bowyer (33) Francois Coquerel (35) Melissa Hung (36-38) Paul Bowyer (39) Michael Kolchesky Photography (40/41) Paul Bowyer

La Rive Gauche (43) Stefan Horn (46) © Musée d'Orsay / Sophie Boegly (47) photograph by Jean de Calan (48) © Musée du quai Branly, photograph by Nicolas Borel (49) © Ron Mueck. Photo © Thomas Salva / Lumento (50) Béatrice Hatala © Beaux-Arts de Paris (51) Martin Geber (52) Paul Bowyer (53) Gabriel de la Chapelle (54) Marc Dantan (55-56) Paul Bowyer (57) Jean-François Chaput

Passy-Étoile (59) Suzanne Levasseur (62) Florent Michel / 11h45 (63) 2013 Artists Rights Society (ARS), New York / ADAGP, Paris / F.L.C.

St Denis-République: (69) Paul Bowyer (71) Martin Gauducheau (72) ICD Bensimon (73-77) Paul Bowyer

La Bastille (79) © Philippe Milbault (82-84) Paul Bowyer (85) F. Flohic (86) Mario Monti

Montmartre & Pigalle (89) Stefan Horn (93) Stéphane Lagoutte (94-98) Paul Bowyer (99) Pascal Martinez

About the Series

—A Modern Take on Simple Elegance

Analogue Guides is a series of curated city guidebooks featuring high quality, unique, low key venues—distilled through the lens of the neighbourhood.

Each neighbourhood is complemented by a concise set of sophisticated listings, including restaurants, cafés, bars, hotels and serendipitous finds, all illustrated with photographs. The listings are supplemented by custom designed, user-friendly maps to facilitate navigation of the cityscape. Venues featured in the guides score high on a number of factors, including locally sourced food, tasteful design, a sophisticated and relaxed atmosphere and independent ownership.

Analogue Guides are designed to complement the internet during pre-travel preparation and smartphones for on-the-ground research. Premium photography and a select choice of venues provide an ideal starting point for pre-travel inspiration. At your destination, the guides serve as portable manuals with detailed neighbourhood maps and clear directions.

The result: a compact, efficient, effervescent manual celebrating the ingenuity of the contemporary metropolis.